INTEGRITY

What Kids Shouldn't Do And Why

by Marvin Soskil
in collaboration with
Abigail and Michael Soskil

Integrity - What Kids Should Do and Why © 2017

Written by Marvin Soskil,

Abigail Soskil and Michael Soskil

Illustrated by Charles Berton

Published by NOI Publishing

All rights reserved.

No parts of this book may be reproduced, digitally or otherwise, without prior written permission from the author.

Visit Marvin Soskil at www.NailofIntegrity.com

Visit Charles Berton at www.charlesberton.com

SPECIAL THANKS to my Grandchildren Abigail and Michael Soskil for inspiring me to write this book. It was our collaboration that brought this to fruition.

WE DEDICATE this book to all the children of the world who need to know that it's okay to be different. It's okay to speak out about the things you feel are not right. I also dedicate this book to parents who need to educate their children as to what is right and what is not.

While speaking to my grandchildren one day, I asked them, "What is *integrity*?"

Abigail was twelve years old and Michael was nine. They said to me, "I don't know, Grandpa. What is integrity?"

I asked them a couple of simple questions to see if they understood, and I asked them to write down all the things kids shouldn't do and why. I said that we should write a book together.

Here is that book...

Hi, we're Isaac Integrity and Nelly the Nail, and we're on a journey to teach you about *integrity*, and to help you understand why it is important to listen to your parents.

Integrity is doing the right thing...when no one is looking.

Role models are people we look up to. They are good people like your parents, your teachers and your pastor. They have special qualities like your favorite athletes andcoaches.

You can turn to people like these because…they have *integrity.*

Police officers and fireman are people you can trust. They are good examples for you to follow.

These people have *integrity*.

Role models are people who have qualities you want to have to be a good person like your teachers, parents and your favorite athlete.

Who else could be a good role model?

Let's talk about some of the things you shouldn't do and why...

When your parents tell you to do something that you don't want to do, do you do it?

"Clean up this room!"

If you don't clean your room... you won't be able to find your favorite toys or favorite clothes."

By doing what you're supposed to do.... That's Integrity.

Your mom baked a whole big tray of cookies and told you that you could not have any cookies until after dinner. If she went downstairs to do the wash, and you knew you could sneak a couple of cookies and no one would know... would you?

Your mom wants you to have room in your belly for good food so you can enjoy the cookies better after dinner. You don't want a stomach ache, do you? Listening to your elders shows *integrity*.

"You should never take any medicine unless your parents give it to you."

Having good sense, that's *integrity*.

If you found a book of matches, you could burn yourself or start a fire.

Never play with fire unless you're supervised by an adult. Being safe, that's *integrity*.

Strangers are people your family doesn't know. No one knows if a stranger is good or bad by looking at them. Some are okay and some might not be. Do not go anywhere with someone you don't know.

Showing common sense...that's *integrity*.

You shouldn't become friends with a stranger or tell things about yourself to someone whom you don't know. You don't know who you might be talking to over the internet.

Your parents allow you to use the internet for playing games and keeping in touch with family and friends. But if you chat with strangers, they might trick you into doing things that are not safe.

Only share things about yourself with people you know. That's *integrity*.

Your parents don't want you to watch scary movies or pictures that are not meant for children, especially when they aren't around.

Scary movies or adult TV programs could cause you to have bad dreams. Programs which are very violent can make you feel uneasy.

Only watch children's show and movies that your parents let you watch. That's *integrity*.

If you saw a cute stay dog, or cat, or any other animal walking down the street, you shouldn't run over to pet it...

...because they might bite or scratch you.
Good judgement shows *integrity*.

It's not a good idea to stick a stick in a hornets' or bees' nest.

If you disturb a bee's nest or a hornet's nest, the bees will come swarming out to protect their nest. You could get stung very badly.

Using good common sense...that's *integrity*.

Bullying or making fun of someone else is not a good thing.

Bullying or ganging up on someone is not a nice thing to do. It makes people feel bad about themselves and about others. Bullies are trouble makers.

If someone bullies you, you should tell an adult so they can help to stop it.

Telling an adult about a bully and protecting someone else... that's *integrity*.

If your parents don't like your friends and tell you to find other friends, you should listen to them. Your parents don't want you to get in trouble. Be safe!

Integrity is doing the right things when nobody is listening or watching. It's being a good person because *you* know the difference.

Everyone can have *integrity!*

Marvin Soskil, author, motivator, mentor, visionary, speaker and entrepreneur has displayed a sense of well being to benefit others. He is a spiritual and community individual, who, as a part of the Long Island Business Community, has raised awareness and funding for many not for profit organizations. As founder of "The Nail of Integrity, LLC" he developed motivational products to sell, but getting the message out became a more rewarding venture. He began writing due to his overwhelming passion for sharing a message and to make a positive impact on society.

His first book, "INTEGRITY... When No One's Looking" (adult) is about doing the right thing in a changing world. Was there ever something that occurred in your lifetime that changed the course of your life's work? For me, it was stepping on a nail. (Available on Amazon in paperback or kindle)

www.NailofIntegrity.com

Made in the USA
Coppell, TX
27 November 2020